NUMBER 654

THE ENGLISH EXPERIENCE

ITS RECORD IN EARLY PRINTED BOOKS
PUBLISHED IN FACSIMILE

31.1.24
20.11.24

(PARLIAMENT)

THE PRIVELEDGES AND PRACTICE OF PARLIAMENTS IN ENGLAND

(LONDON), 1628

WALTER J. JOHNSON, INC.
THEATRUM ORBIS TERRARUM, LTD
AMSTERDAM 1974 NORWOOD, N.J.

The publishers acknowledge their gratitude to
the Curators of the Bodleian Library, Oxford,
for their permission to reproduce the Library's
copy, Shelfmark: $4°$.C.80 Th (8); and page A_1 r
from the Library's copy, Shelfmark: A.10.24, and
pages B_2 v, B_3 r, B_4 v and D_4 r from the Library's
copy, Shelfmark: $4°$.E.1.Jur.(8)

S.T.C. No. 7749

Collation: A-F^4, G^2

Published in 1974 by

Theatrum Orbis Terrarum, Ltd.
O.Z. Voorburgwal 85, Amsterdam

&

Walter J. Johnson, Inc.
355 Chestnut Street
Norwood, New Jersey
07648

Printed in the Netherlands

ISBN 90 221 0654 3

Library of Congress Catalog Card Number:
74-80218

THE
PRIVILEDGES
AND PRACTICE
OF
PARLIAMENTS
IN
ENGLAND.

Collected out of the Common
Lawes of this Land.

*Seene and allowed by the Learned in
the Lawes.*

COMMENDED
To the High Court of Parliament
now Assembled.

Printed. 1628.

The principall Contents of this ensuing Discourse.

A 3   10 *Knights*

The Contents.

A

A discourse of the Priuiledge and practice of the high Court of Parliament in England, colleĕed out of the Common-Lawes of this Land.

He moſt Common and beſt meanes for the preſervation and Conſerva-tion aſwell of private as publique Tranquilitie and Societie vſed in all Ages, and by all Nations, is by way of lawfull Aſſembly, and Con-ſultation, which wee call *Parlia-ment*, to looke into the neceſſitie of publique Condition, and ſo to fore-ſee ſeaſonable re-medie.

Where no Counſell is, the people fall, But where many Counſellers are, there is health, Prou. 11, and 14. *Tul-ly* ſaith, *Communis vtilitatis de relictio contra naturam eſt*. The Saxons called this Court *Miclegemot*, the great Aſſembly, and *Witenagemot*, the Aſſemblie of wiſe-men; The Latine Authors of thoſe times called it *Commune Conſilium, magna curia generalis conventus, &c.* But W i l l i a m the Conquerour as it ſeemeth changed the name of this Court, and firſt called it by

the

the name of *Parleament*. But manifeſt it is, that the Conquerour changed not the frame or Iuriſdiction of this Court in any point; yea, the very names which are attributed to this Court before the Conqueſt are continued after the Conqueſt to this day. And where ſome doe ſuppoſe, That in the Parliament holden at *Weſtminſter* in the 3. *Ed.* 1 called *Weſtminſter* the firſt, the word *Parliament* firſt crept in where it is called the firſt generall *Parliament* by the aſſent, of the Arch-biſhops, Biſhops, Abbots, Earles, Barons, and all the Communaltie of the Land ſummoned to the ſame; yet it is manifeſt that the name of *Parliament* was long before that time, and for proofe thereof note: 21. *Fd. Fol.* 60. and in Sir *Edward Coke* Preface to his 9th. Booke, where it is fully proued; That the Conquerour himſelfe did hold this Parliament, and other his mediate Succeſſors. Although in the bookes of Statutes mention is not made of any Statute before *Magna Charta*, in the 9th. yeare of *Hen* 3.

And this is not that Court, which in *France* bea-reth the name of *Parliament*, for they are but ordinary Courts of Iuſtice; But this is that Court which both *England* and *Scotland* agreeth in naming it *Parliament*, which the *French* call. *Aſſemble de eſtates*, or *Les eſtates*. And the *Germanes*, *A Rikes Daggh*, or *Dyet*.

Of this Court it may be ſayd, *Si vetuſtatem ſpectes eſt antiquiſſima, ſi dignitatem eſt honoratiſſima, ſi juriſdi-ctionem eſt copioſiſſima*. And as Sir *Edward Coke* obſer-ueth in his Preface to his 9. Booke. This great and Ho-nourable aſſembly hath a Three-fold end; Firſt, that the Subiect might be kept from offending, that is, that offences might be prevented, both by good and pro-
vident

vident Lawes & by due execution of them. Secondly,
that men might liue fafely in quiet ; And thirdly, that
all men might receiue Iuftice by certaine Lawes and
holy Iudgement. To the end that Iuftice might be the
better adminiftred , That queftions and defects in
Law. by this high Court of Parliament : be explained
and brought to certainty and judgement.

Our Soueraigne King *Charles* in his late Proclamation calls it , *The great Councell of Vs and Our
Kingdome.*

And torafmuch as this *great* and *principall Court* is
the Kings Court , and the Court of the Kingdome
whereof the King is fupreame head and gouernour ,
neither the Lords nor the Commons can fummon it
nor appoint any certaine time or place for the Affem-
blie of the Parliament; For that onely doth appertaine
to the King to doe. See the Statute 2 1. *R:c.*2.*Ca.*1 2.
And in the Kings name onely fuch fummons muft be
made as an abfolute Prerogatiue incident to his
Crowne and Dignity. Like as diuers things do folely
belong to the King, whereof the Subiect hath nothing
to do : as *fœdera Percurere* to make Leagues, or *bellum
incidere,* 9. *Ed.*4 *fol,*6. The King onely without the
Subiect , may make letters of *Denifation* , to whom
and how many he will. And the King by his Proclamation may make any Coine lawfull money of England : And many other things doe appertaine to the
King as fpeciall flowers of his Crowne.

And if the King happen to be in any forreine part,
yet the Parliament holden in this Realme in the Kings
abfence muft be fummoned in the Kings name vnder
the *Teftu* of the Kings *Lieutenant,*as by the Statute 8.
Hen. 5, *Ca.*1. may appeare.

B   *Bracton*

Bracton faith , Parliaments haue beene holden by
the Kings Lieutenant Procurator or Deputy, as in the
13.*Ed*.2.the King conftituted *Adomarum de Valen-
tia Comitem Pembrocia cuftodem, Regni fui, & locum
fuum tenendum quamdiu Rex in partibus tranfmarinis
moram fecerit.*

And the Kings of this Land haue conftituted as
their Lieutenants or Deputies to fummon the Parliament 3. or 4. in a Commifsion as in the 24, of *Hen.*8.
at his being at *Callice* a Parliament was holden by
commifsion as followeth :

Henricus 8. *Dei gratia Anglia , Francia, Rex fidei
defenfor: Dominus Hibernia Reuerendiffimo in Chrifto
Patri Edwardo Archiepifcopo , Eborac. Predelicto &
fideli fuo Thome Audeley Militi, duo Cuftodi Magni
Sigilli , ac Chariffimo confanguineo fuo Roberto Comiti
Suffex falutem : Cum Prefens Parliamentum noftrum a-
pud Ciuitatem noftram London.3.die Nouembris, anno
Regni noftri viceffimo primo in Choat. & vfque Weftm.
Prorogat , & ibidem poft diuerfas continuationes &
Prorogationes idem Parliamentum noftrum apud Weft-
minftr. 14. diem Nouembris apud Weftminft. etiam
Prorogat. fuerat. Ibidem tunc tenendum nos idcirco con-
fiderante abfentiam noftram a regno noftro Anglia apud
Calice exiftent in caufis vrgentiffimis nos & Rem Pub-
licam regni noftri , concernent alysq, Confederationibus
nos fpecialitur mouentibus ac de fidelitate , integritate ,
induftria & circumfpectione veftris plenus confidentes,
de aduifamento & affenfu confily noftri affigiamus vos &
duos veftrum Dantes vobis & duobus veftrum plenam
Poteftatem, facultatem, & authoritatem, hac inftante
die lune ad & in quartum diem Februar. Prox. futurum vfq, Weftm. Predictum Prorogandum & con-
tinuan-*

sinuandum ibidem tunc tenendum. Et idio vobis man-
damus quod circa premissa diligenter intendatis, ac ea in-
forma predict.effectualiter expleatis. Damus autem vni-
uersis & singulis Archiepiscopus, Episcop. Abib. Prior.
Duabus, Marchionib.Committibus, Vicecommit.Baro-
nibus, Militib.Ciuibus, Burgensib.ab omnibus, alijs quo-
rum interest aut intere potent. in hac parte : in mandatis
quod ipsi omnes, &c. Singula in premissis omnibus sin-
gulis faciendum & exequendum intendentes fuit confu-
lentes & obedientes prout decet. In cunis rei Testimo-
nium has literas nostras fieri fecimus Patentes. Teste
me ipso apud Westm.4. Die Nouembris, anno regni nostri
vicesimo quarto.

Penals.

And a King in possession of his Kingdome during
his raigne may before his Coronation summon his
Parliament as taking one example in a case so cleere
for all : King *Hen.* 6. was not crowned vntill the 8.
yeare of his raigne, and yet in his 1, 2, 3, 4, 5, and
6. yeare of his raigne diuers Parliaments were holden, (as also our gratious Soueraigne King *Charles,*
called a Parliament *Anno* 1. before his Coronation.)
And summoned by him *Hen.* 6. as in the Statutes may
appeare : For it is cleerely resolued by all the Iudges
of England, that presently by discent he is absolutely
and compleately King without any essentiall ceremo-
nie or act to be done *ex post facto*, and that Coronation is but a royall ornament or outward solemniza-
tion of the discent, And the King is as absolute and
compleate a King both for matter of Iudicatorie as
Graunts, &c. both before his Coronation as hee was
after.

Also

Alfo the King being within age, may afwell fummon his Parliament as if hee were at full age, as by the example was feene in the faid *Hen.6.* & *Ed.6.* and obferue the cafe of the Dutchie of *Lancafter in Plowdens Commentaries,* 2 2 1 .6. Where it is agreed, that the perfon of the King is not infeebled by his nonage, for his perfon doth alwaies remaine of full age, afwell to make guifts and graunts as in adminiftration of Iuftice.

And the diuerfity of Sex maketh no difference as by the Statute made in the firft yeare of Queene *Mary* holden by Prorogation *Can : 1.* is declared.

Alfo a King being in poffefsion of his Kingdome whether by rightfull title or by wrong as an *Vfurper.* He is a perfon able *Ipfo facto* to fummon a Parliament, as by the example holden by *Hen.6.* before and after the redemption of his Crowne being remoued therefrom by *Ed.4.* wherein the faid *Edward* was in his Remitter as is to bee feene in *Baggots* afsife, in the *9.* yeare of *Ed.4.* fol. 1.6. *& fequentium* whereby it is faid, that *Hen : 6.* was King in poffefsion. And it was neceffary that the Realme haue a King vnder whom the Lawes may be holden and maintained. And therefore though he was but vfurpation, yet euery act Iudicially done by him, which doth concerne his Iurifdiction Royall fhall be good, and bind the rightfull King his regreffe, and diuers other Examples there are hereof. See 1 *.Hen.7.* fol. 3.

In ancient times after the King had fummoned his Parliament to be holden at a certaine day and place, Innumerable multitudes of people did make their acceffe thereunto, pretending that priuiledge of right to belong to them, And not onely to the Lords fpirituall

all and Temporall but alſo to the Commonalty being
Freeholders : But King *Hen.* 3. hauing had experi-
ence of the miſchiefes and inconueniences by occaſi-
on of ſuch popular confuſion, did take order and re-
ſtrayned that ouer great acceſſe, So that none might
come to his Parliament but thoſe who were ſpecially
ſummoned , which his ſonne *Edw.* 1. did carefully
keepe and obſerue, according to that auncient ſaying,
Ad Conſilium ne acceſſeris antequam voceris. And ſo
euer ſince this ſpeciall manner of ſummons of Parliament now vſed hath beene put in Practiſe. The vſu-
all forme of ſummons for the Parliament for the Commonaltie, is not ſpeciall, but a generall Writ is directed to the Sheriffe of euery Countie or Shire in *England* and *Wales*, in this forme.

Rex vice. N. *Salutem quia de adviſamento & aſ-*
ſenſum Conſilÿ noſtri quibuſdam arduis & vrgentibus
negotÿs nos Statum & defenſionem Regni noſtri Angliæ,
& Eccleſ. Anglicanè concernent quandam Parliamen-
tum noſtrum apud Civitatem noſtram Weſtm. 17. die
Martÿ Prox. futurum teneri ordinavimus & ibidem
cum Prelatibus magnatibus & proceribus dicti Regni
noſtri colloquium Habere, & tractare, Tibi Precipimus
firmiter iniungentes quod facta Proclamacionè in Prox.
com. tuo poſt receptionem hujus brevis noſtri tenendum
die & loco Predicto. duos Milites, gladÿs tinctis ma-
gis idonios & diſcretos cum predict. &c. Et Electionem
illam in pleno com. tuo factū diſtinctè & aparte, ſub Si-
gillo tuo & ſigillis eorum qui Electioni illi inter fuerunt,
nobis in Cancellariam noſtram ad dictum diem & locum
certifices indilate, Teſte meipſo, &c. vide Statut. 23.
H.6. Ca. 15.

And

And concerning thoſe of *Wales* to be ſummoned to the Parliament, read the Statute thereof 27. *Hen.* 8. *Can.* 26. Intituled, *an act for Lawes and Iuſtice to be miniſtred in Wales,* in like forme as it is in this Realme. And alſo that other Statute made 35. *Hen.*8. *Can.*11. Intituled an *Act for the due payment of Fees and Wages of Knights and Burgeſſes of the Parliament, in Wales,* And thereof ſee in *Plowdens Comentaries* 120. Sir *Richard Bulkleyes* Caſe, and in *Dyer* 13.

And concerning thoſe of the County Palatine of *Cheſter,* and of the City of *Cheſter* in this behalfe, ſee the Statute made 34. *Hen.*8.*Can.*13.

In *Anno* 1. of Queene *Mary* a great doubt was moued amongſt the Iuſtices and Serieants, If the Queenes writ of ſummons of the Parliament in which the Stile or title of *Supremum Caput Eccleſia Anglicana.* were omitted, were good and ſufficient or vtterly voide,&c. Becauſe the ſaid Stile is vnited and annexed by the Statute made the 26. and 35. *Hen.*6. to the Imperiall Crowne of the Realme. But the greater opinion was, ſuch ſummons is good enough, for they ſaid that *Supremum Caput* is not parcell of the Queenes name, but an addition, and the words in the Statute are onely in the affirmatiue and not negatiuely, That the Stile ſhall be of neceſſity ſo written of the Queene. And this doubt was by Queene *Elizabeth* againe moued in the firſt Parliament, and was aduiſed and reſolued by great aduice and deliberation (*vt ſupra*) ſee the Statute 1. and 2. of *Phil.* and *Ma. Ca.* 8. And in Maſter *Foxes* Acts and Monuments ſo: The argument of *John Hales* to the contrary, *cuiuſcunque poteſſima Pars eſt Principium,* which Rule is expreſſed in Sir *Edward Cokes* 10. part 49. 1. but *ibidem fol.* 161.

161. *a.* the Ancient rule is cited, *Qui libet poeeβ renun-ciare Iuris Pro ſe introductʒa.*

At euery County after the deliuery of the Parliament writ to the Sheriffes, Proclamation ſhalbe made in the full County of the day and place of the Paliament, and that all men ſhall attaine for election of the Knights for the ſame County for the Parliament, The which Knights muſt be reſident within the ſame County, whereof they are to be choſen the day of the the writ of ſummons of the Parliament, whereof euery one ought to haue 40. s. of Free-hold within the ſaid County beyond all charges. And ſuch who haue the greateſt number of the ſaid Electors, ſhalbe returned Knights for the ſame County, ſee 7. *Hen.* 4. *Ca.* 12.1. *Hen.* 6. *Ca.* 1. 8. *Hen.* 6. *Can.* 13. and 10. *Hen.* 6. *Can.* 7.

The Sheriffe may examine euery one of the ſaid Electors vpon the ſaid Euangeliſts, how much he may diſpend by yeare if he doubt of the value thereof, 8. *Hen.* 6. *Can.* 7.

The ſaid election ſhall be made in the full County betweene the houres of 8. and 9. before noone; 23. *Hen.* 6. *Can.* 15.

The ſaid Knights ſhall bee returned into the Chancery by Indenture, ſealed betweene the Sheriffe and the ſaid Electors, 8. *H.* 6. *Ca.* 7. 7. *H.* 4. *Ca.* 1. 23. *H.* 6. *Can.* 6. *vt patet per breue ſupra.*

Every Sheriffe who doth not make a true returne of ſuch election of Knights to come to the Parliament according to the Statute in that behalfe made, that is to ſay; The Statute 8. *H.* 6. *Ca.* 7. ſhall forfeit 100ˡ. to the King, and 100ˡ to the Knight ſo choſen, who ſhall Commence his action within 3. moneths after the Parlia-

Parliament commenced. And if hee fo doe not and profecute his fuite in effect and without fraud : Any other man who will may haue the faid fuite, for the faid 100¹. as the Knight had, and cofts of fuit alfo fhall be awarded to the faid Knight or other who will fue in his behalfe, 23. *Hen. 6. Ca. 15.*

No Sheriffe fhall be chofen for a Knight of the Parment nor for a Burgeffe, fee the booke of Entries 411. And at a Parliament holden 38. *Hen. 8.* It was admitted and accepted that if a Burgeffe of the Parliament bee made Maior of a Towne, or haue Iudiciall Iurifdiction, or another is ficke, That thefe are caufes fufficient to thofe others. And fo was done by the Kings writ out of the Chancery, comprehending this matter which was in *Commune domo Parliamenti, 7. and 38. Hen. 8.*

In euery writ of Parliament directed to the Sheriffe, this claufe fhall be inferted : *Electionem tuam in pleno Com. tuo factum distincte & aperte sub Sigillo tuo & Sigillis eorum qui electioni illi inter fuerunt nos in Cancellariam nostram ad diem & locum in breue Content. certifices indilato :* Hen. 4. *Can. 15.*

The Sheriffe after the receipt of the writ of Election, &c. fhall deliuer without fraud a fufficient precept vnder his feale to euery Maior, and Bayliffe or Bayliffes where no Maior is, of City and Burrough within his County, reciting in his precept the writ of Parliament, commanding them by the faid precept; If it be a City to thofe Citizens for the fame City by Citizens, And if it be a Burrough then Burgèffes, by Burgeffes of the fame to come to the Parliament. And

And that the said Maior, or Bayliffe, or Bayliffes, where no Maior is, shall returne lawfully the said precept to the Sheriffe : and those who made the Elections, and of the names of the said Citizens & Burgesses by them so chosen : 23.*Hen*.6.*Ca*.15.

The Sheriffe shall make a good returne of his writ, and of euery returne of the Maior and Bayliffe or Bayliffes , or Bayliffes where no Maior is to him made. And if the Sheriffe doe contrary to this Statude made for the election of Knights, Citizens, and Burgesses to come to the Parliament, he shall incurre the paine of 100.pounds to the King, and shall bee imprisoned for one whole yeare, without Bayle or maine-price. And the Knight for the County returned contrary to the said ordinance, shall loose their wages by the Statute, 8. *Hen*. 6.*Can*. 7. And the Sheriffe shall loose 100.pounds to euery Knight, Citizen, and Burgesse, chosen in his County to come to the Parliament; And not duely returned , or to any other who will sue in his default by action of Debt, with costs expended in that case : In which suite, the defendant shall not wage Law, nor be essoyned, *Anno* 23. *Hen*.6. *Can*. 15.

If the Maior, and Bayliffe, or Bayliffes, or Bayliffes where no Maior is, doe returne others then those who be chosen by the Citizens and Burgesses of the Cities and Boroughs , where such Election shall bee made , hee shall forfeit to the King 40.pounds, and so much to the Citizen or Burgesse chosen to come to the Parliament and not duely returned by the Maior or Bayliffe, or Bayliffes where no Maior

is,

is, or to any other perſon who in default of ſuch Citizen or Burgeſſe ſo choſen, will ſue for it by action of debt with coſts expended. And they ſhall haue a writ of debt for the ſaid 40. pounds, in which the defendant ſhall not wage his Law nor ſhall be eſſoyned, 23 . Hen. 6. Can. 1 5.

Euery Knight, Citizen, or Burgeſſe, choſen and not returned, ſhall Commence his action within 3. Moneths next after the commencing of the ſaid Parliament, in which he muſt proceede effectually without fraud, And if he ſo doe not, any other who will ſue for it, ſhall haue the ſaid Action for the ſaid Forfeiture, and coſts in the ſame expended : in which the Defendant ſhall not wage Law, nor ſhalbe eſſoyned, Anno 23. Hen. 6. Can. 1 5.

If any Knight, Citizen, or Burgeſſe, that ſhall bee returned by the Sheriffe to come to the Parliament, be after ſuch returne put out, and another put in his place, hee that is in his place ſo put out, if hee take vpon him to bee a Knight, Citizen, or Burgeſſe, ſhall forfeite to the King 1 00, pounds, and ſo much to the Knight, Citizen, or Burgeſſe, returned by the Sheriffe : and ſo afterwards put out, and the ſame Knight, Citizen, or Burgeſſe, ſo put out, ſhall haue an action of debt againſt him ſo put in his place, his Executors and adminiſtrators, and ſhall commence his action within 3. Moneths after the beginning of the Parliament : and if he ſue not as before, any other who will, ſhall haue the ſame ſuit : in which the Defendant ſhall not wage his law, nor ſhall bee eſſoyned ; ſo that ſuch Knight of the Parliament choſen,

(13)

chofen, be a Knight or fuch Efquire or Gentleman of
the fame County, who may bee a Knight, and none
to bee fuch a Knight, who ftands in the Degree of
a Yeoman: *Anno* 23. *Hen.* 6. *Can.* 15.

All perfons and Commonalties who fhall be fummoned to the Parliament, fhall come as it hath beene
accuftomed of the Ancient time : And hee that commeth not, hauing no reafonable excufe fhall bee a-
merced, and otherwife punifhed as of Ancient time
hath beene vfed, 5. *R.* 2. *Statut.* 2. *Ca.* 4.

If any Archbifhop, Bifhop, Duke, Marquis,
Earle or Baron, be fummoned by the Kings writ to
come to the Parliament and thorough ficknes or any
other infirmitie hee cannot make his appearance at
the faid Parliament, hee muft procure from the King
his Warrant of abfence, as in like cafe was granted
to the Abbot of *Eufham* in the 23. yeare of *Hen.* 8.
in forme following,

H. 8.

By the King.

Trufty and welbeloued, Wee greet you well, and albe-
it you haue monition among other Prelates of our Realme
to bee prefent at our high Court of Parliament to bee
holden : yet neuerthelefse Wee of our efpeciall grace con-
fidering your debility and age, bee content and by thefe
prefents Licence you to bee abfent from our faid Parlia-
ment during the continuance, prorogation, or adiorn-
ment of the fame : The faid Monition, or any other

C 2   *writ*

writ directed to you, or Commandement giuen by vs to
you notwithstanding vnder our Seale, signed at our
Mannor of Greenwich, *The 6. of Ianuary in the 23.*
of our raigne.

To our trustie and welbeloued in
God, the Abbot of our Monaste-
ry of *Eusham.*

And it appeareth to be true which *Fortescue* saith
in his 18. *Can. Fol.* 40. That Acts of Parliament
and Statutes in England, are not made onely by the
Princes pleasure, but also by the consent of the whole
Realme : So that of necessity they must procure the
Weale of the whole Realme, and in no wise tend to
their hinderance. And it cannot bee otherwise
thought but that they are replenished with much wit
and wisedome, seeing they are not ordained by the
aduice of one man onely, or of a 100. wise Councellors, but of more then 300. chosen men, which
agreeth with the ancient number of ancient Senators
of Rome.

No Baron, Knight, Citizen or Burgesse, who shalbe
chosen to come to the Parliament, shall not depart
vntill that Parliament be ended or prorogued if he haue
not licenfe of the Speaker, and of the Commons as-
sembled in that Parliament, which licenfe shalbe en-
tred in the Booke of the Clearke of the Parliament appointed for the *Lower House,* vpon paine of losing their
wages, whereof all Counties and Burroughes shall
be discharged, *6. Hen. 8. Can. 16.*

Con-

Concerning the due leauying of Knights Fees and wages for attendance at the Parliament, see the Statute made 23. *Hen. 6. Can.* 11.

Knights and Burgesses for the Parliament must take the *Oath of Allegiance*, and so shall Citizens and Barons for the Fiue Ports, for the Parliament before they doe enter into the Parliament house *Anno* 5. *Eliz. Ca.* 1. and they must also take the *Oath of Supremacie*, made 7. *Iacobi Can.* 6. Which two Oathes shall be taken before the Lord Steward for the time being, or his Deputy or Deputies.

Memorandum in the Statute made, *Anno* 25. *Hen.* 8. *Can.* 19. Intituled an Act concerning the submifsion of the Clergie of the Kings Maieftie, is contained, that the Conuocation is and alwaies hath bin and ought to be aftembled by the Kings writ, The forme whereof is thus set downe by Doctor *Cowell* in his Interpreter *Verbo Proclam.* First, the King directeth his writ to the Archbifhop of each Prouince, for the fummoning of all Bifhops, Deanes, Archdeacons, Cathedrall and Collegiate Churches, and generally all the Clergie of his Frouince: after their beft difcretions and judgements, afsigning to them the time and place in the faid writ, Then the Archbifhops proceede in their accuftomed courfe one example may fhew both. The Archbifhop of *Canterbury* vpon his writ of fummons receiued, directeth his letters to the Bifhop of *London* as his Deane Prouinciall: Firft citing him peremptorily, And then willing him to Seite in like manner all the Bifhops,

Deanes,

Deanes, Arch Deacons, Cathedrall and Colegiate Churches, and generally all the Clergie of his Prouince, to the place and againſt the day prefixed in the writ, but directeth withall : That one Proctor ſent for euery Cathedrall or Collegiate Church, and two for the body of the inferior Clergie of each Dioceſſe may ſuffice, and by vertue of theſe Letters Authentically ſealed. The ſaid Biſhop of *London* ſendeth the like Letters ſeuerally to the Biſhops of euery Dioceſſe of the Prouince, cyting them in like manner. And commandeth them not onely to appeare, but alſo to admoniſh the ſaid Deanes and Archdeacons, perſonally to appeare, and the Cathedrall and Collegiate Churches, alſo of the common *Clergie* of the Dioceſſe, to ſend their Proctors at the day appointed in the Writ : And alſo will them to certifie the Archbiſhop, the names of all and euery one ſo ſummoned by them, in a ſchedule annexed to their Letters Certificatorie. The Biſhops proceed accordingly, and the Cathedrall and Collegiate Churches: as alſo the Clergie make choiſe of their Proctors, which done and certified to the Biſhop, he returneth all Anſwerable to his charge, (*Caue lector*) for the *Clergie* of the Conuocation houſe, are no part or member of the Parliament : as you may ſee reſolued by the Lord *Richard* Lord *Winſor*, and others ; in the beginning of the ſixt Examination of Maſter *Philpot*, in the beginning of the raigne of Queene *Mary* : in Maſter *Foxes* booke of Martyrs, *Fol.* 16,9 cantrary to the opinion of Doctor *Cowell, vbi ſupra*. Neuertheleſſe it is enacted by the Statute 8. *Hen.* 6. *Can.* 1. That all the Clergie called to the Conuocation houſe by the Kings writ, and their ſeruants and familiars ſhall haue and

fully

fully vſe euery ſuch libertie and defence in comming, abiding, and going, as the Great men and
commonaltie of the Land) to bee called to the Parliament of the King ſh all haue.

And becauſe mention is here made of the Priuiledges appertaining to thoſe of the Parliament-
houſe; take heere a word or two thereof. The
Words of the Statute made the 11. *Hen. 6. Can.* 11.
are as followeth : The King willing to prouide for
eaſe and tranquility of thoſe that come to his Parliament: Hath ordained and eſtabliſhed, That if any
aſſault or affray be made vpon any Lord Spirituall or
Temporall, Knight of the Shire, Citizen or Burgeſſe, comming to the Parliament, or the Councell
of our Soueraigne Lord the King. That then Proclamation ſhall be made, in the moſt open place of the
City or Towne where the affray was ſo made, by
3. ſeuerall dayes, That the partie that made ſuch affray
and aſſault, yeild himſelfe before the King and his
Bench, within a quarter of a yeare after the proclamation ſo made, if it be in the time of the Terme, or o-
therwiſe in the next day in the time of the Terme
following the ſaid quarter. And if he ſo doe not, that
he bee attainted of the deede, and pay to the partie
greeued his double damages, to bee taxed at the diſcretion of the Iuſtices of the ſame Bench for the time
being, or by inqueſt if it be needfull, and make Fine
and Ranſome at the Kings will, and if he come and
be found guiltie by inqueſt, examination or otherwiſe
of ſuch affray or aſſault, then hee ſhall pay vnto the
partie greeued thereby, his double damages found
by the Inqueſt, or to be taxed by the diſcretion of the
Iuſtices,

Iuſtices , and make Fine and Ranſome at the will and pleaſure of our Soueraigne Lord the King.

Euery Knight, Citizen , Burgeſſe , Baron of the Fiue Ports or others , called to the Parliament of the King; Shall haue priuiledge of the Parliament during the Seſſions of Parliament , ſo that he that doth arreſt any of them during that time , ſhall bee impriſoned in the Tower by the Nether Houſe , of which he is and ſhall be put to his fine and the Keeper alſo , if he will not deliuer him when the Serjant at Armes doth come for him by the commandement of the houſe whereof hee is : See *Dyer,*60.

The ſeruants attending vpon their Maſters during Parliament who are neceſſary , and alſo ſuch Officers as bee attending vpon the Parliament , as the Serieant at Armes , the Porter of the doore, Clearks and ſuch like , and in the ſame manner of their chattells and goods neceſſary , ſo that they ſhall not bee arreſted nor taken by any Officer , if it bee not in caſe of Fellony or Treaſon , in the ſame manner , as the Iudges and Miniſters of other Courts ſhall haue for their Seruants , goods and chattells neceſſary , See *Cromptons Courts,*fol.11. a.

But the Parliament doth not giue priuiledge *Tempore vacationis ſed Scedente curia.* See *Brooks title priuiledge* , 56. It appeareth that in the Parliament ₁. *Hen.* 6. in the vacation , the Parliament being continued by Prorogation , *Thomas Thorpe* the Speaker was condemned in a Thouſand markes , damages by an Action of Treſpaſſe brought againſt him

him by the Duke of *Yorke*, and was committed to prison in Execution for the same, and after when the Parliament was re-assembled, the Commons made suite to the King and Lordes to haue *Thorpe* their Speaker, deliuered for the good exployte of the Parliament: whereupon the Dukes Councell declared the whole cause at large, whereupon the Lords demanded the opinion of the Iudges, whether in that case, *Thorpe* ought to bee deliuered out of prison by priuiledge of Parliament; The Iudges made this answere, that they ought not to determine the priuiledge of that high Court of Parliament: But for Declarations of proceedings in Law, Courts in case where writs of *Superfedias* for the priuiledge of the Parliament be brought vnto them, they answer; That if any person that is a member of the Parliament be arrested in such case as it be not for Treason or Fellony, or for surety of the Peace, or for condemnation had before the Parliament, It is vsed that such persons be released and may make Attorney, so as they may haue their freedome and liberty freely to attend that Parliament: Hereupon it was concluded, That *Thorpe* should still remaine in prison according to the Law. Notwithstanding, the priuiledge of Parliament, and that he was the Speaker, which resolution was declared to the Commons by *Walter Moile* one of the Kings Serieants at Law, and then the Commons were commanded in the Kings name by the Bishop of *Lincolne*, in the Absence of the Arch-Bishop of *Canterbury* then Chancellor, to choose another Speaker.

It

It hath beene much doubted whether one taken in Execution during the Parliament, may be set
at liberty by writ of Parliament, as is to be seene in
the first of *Eliz. 4. Fol. 8. a. Dyer, 60.* But at this
day the Law is explained in that case by the Statute
made, *1. Iacob. Can. 19.* Intituled *an act for new execution to be sued against any who shall hereafter be deliuered out of prison by priuiledge of Parliament. And
for discharge of them out of whose custody such prisoners
shall be deliuered.*

The forme of a Protection to be made by any person
of eyther House of Parliament, vnto such of their
Servants as may stand in danger of Arresting in
time of Parliament.

*Whereas by the ancient Priuiledges, Lawes and Cu-
stomes of this Realme heretofore vsed and approued.
The Lords Spirituall and Temporall, the Knights, Citizens and Burgesses of the Parliament, haue alwayes
had their seruants and followers priuiledged and free
from any molestation, trouble, arrest or imprisonment,
for some certaine dayes, both before the beginning and
after the ending of the same. And wher as at this time
a Parliament is summmoned where my selfe being a Baron and Peere of the Realme (or Knight, or Burgesse)
and there to make my appearance. I vnderstand notwithstanding, that you or some of you, haue now in your
hands some Processe, Writ or Warrant, to molest, arrest, imprison I. B. my houshold Seruant in ordinary,*
                                                      whose

Whofe attendance I haue fpeciall caufe to vfe and employ
in matters which doe much concerne and import my e-
ftate, and other occafions to bee followed and folicited by
him during this Seffions of Parliament. Thefe are therefore to Charge and Command you, and euery one of you,
both to withdraw the fame Proceffe, Writ or Warrant,
if any fuch bee ; As alfo, if thereby you or any of you,
haue molefted, arrefted, or imprifonea him the faid I. B.
within the Compaffe of the forefaid dayes of priuiledge ;
That then vpon fight hereof, you prefently fet him at Libertie, as you or any of you will anfwere the contrary.
Giuen vnder my hand and Seale the 16. day of Februa-
ry, 1627.

        To all Maiors, Sheriffes, Bayliffes, Sergeants,
        Knights, Marfhals-men, and all other
        his Maiefties Officers.

R S.

The forme of a Letter to bee directed to the Sheriffe of *L.* for difcharge of a Seruant that is
Arrefted vpon Execution, and during the time
of the Parliament notwithftanding his Protection.

*Mr. Sheriffe, whereas I was to bee attended to the
Parliament, I wanted one of my houfhold feruants, a
Gentleman of mine, called B. to whom I had giuen a
priuiledge for this Seffion of Parliament, to preuent any
arreft or imprifonment for his debts, to the end he might
waite on mee, and profecute my bufines with more di-
ligence and leffe danger of Interruption in that kinde.
But I now vnderftand hee is in the Cuftody of the Sheriffe of* Middlefex, *within the dayes limitted vpon an
Execution of* 1000. *pounds, And that hee doth deraine
him and will take no notice of my priuiledge vnder my
hand and Seale, although it hath beene fhewed him:
I haue chofen rather to write to you then to take the
Ancient priuiledges and liberties of the vppermoft
Houfe of Parliament, and the honour of a Peere of this
Kingdome into your friendly confideration, then that I
would be offenfiue to any your fubordinate Officers, in
fending for them and the Plaintiffe by a Serieant at
Armes, Or to conuent them before the Lords for their
contempt. And Mr. Sheriffe, i am further giuen to
vnderftand, that the Deputy is brother to the vnder-
Sheriffe, and that hee did execute the Office the laft
yeare, which is a plaine defrauding of the Law, not*
                                                    being

being three yeares betwixt them, being well knowne that his brother doth not intermeddle in the Office at all, nor taketh any notice at all what Warrants are made foorth in his name, or of what Writs are brought to his hands, for his Deputie doth take the whole benefit of the place into his owne hands. And by this meanes the vnder Sheriffe being in Glocestershire, *hee hath a collour as his Deputy not to take notice of our priuiledges being directed to the Sheriffe; herewith I thought good to acquaint you, expecting your answere and the releafe of my Seruant, otherwise, I purpose not to loose the priuiledge of a Peere of the Realme, whilest it concernes our honour. And is no Indempnity to the Plaintiffe, whose Judgement and Execution is in as much force and strength, by a late Statute to take hold of* B. *afterwards as it was before.*

Concerning the vpper houfe of Parliament; firſt it is obſerued, that thither commeth all Lords of the Parliament aſwell Spirituall as Temporall, and they are ſummoned by the Kings writ alſo, but *Separatim*, and not by a generall writ to the Sheriffe of the County, as the Commons are ſummoned who

are

are of the lower house of the Parliament, the forme of which writ is as followeth.

Carolus, &c. Charissimo consanguineo suo comiti Oxford Quia de aduisamento & assensu Consily nostri, Pro quibusdam arduis & vrgentibus negotys nos Statut. & defensionem Regni nostri & Ecclef. Anglicanis concernent quandam Parliamentum nostrum apud Ciuitate nostram Westm. 12. die Martij, Prox.futur. teneri ordinauimus, & ibidem vobiscum ac cum Prelatibus magnatibus & proceribus dicti Regni nestri Colloquum habere & tractare; vobis sub fide & legeancys quibus nobis tenenum firmiter iniungentes Mandamus quod considerationem dictorum negotiorum arduate & periculis in mentibus Cessante executione quicurq, dicto die & loco personaliter interfitis nobiscum, ac cum Prelatibus magnatibus & proceribus supradictis negotijs, tractare vestrumq, consilium impensur. Et hoc ficut nos & honorem nostram, & rempublicam, & saluationem, & defensionem Regni & Ecclesia, predict. expedicionemq, negotiorum dictorum diligitis nulla tenus omittatis. Teste me ipsa apud Westm. 18. die Ianuarij Anno Regni nostri, &c.

At the first day appointed by the King for the Parment vsually the King in person doth ride thither as it were to open the dore of their Authoritie, attended by all the Lords Spirituall and Temporall in their Parliament Roabes. But if the King be let *per Egritudinem* or by other Causes, his Maiestie may command the adiornement of the Parliament to be held at some other day at his pleasure, as was done at the first day of the Parliament holden the first yeare of

the

the late Queene *Eliz.* as appeareth in *Dyer, Fol.* 20. 3. *a* : Which Parliament was prorogued by writ Patent, vnder their entire great Seale and fignet with the hand of the Queeene : by which Booke the printed Booke of the Statutes may be corrected.

And the King may vnder his great Seale afsigne 2. or 3. of the Lords of the Parliament to fupply his place in Parliament, if he be ficke or will not come for any other caufe, *vt factum fuit, Anno* 31. *Eliz.* At which time the Archbifhop of *Canterbury*, The Lord Treafurer of *England*, and the Earle of *Derby*, were Commifsioners, vnder the great Seale appointed and afsigned to reprefent her Maiefties perfon in Parliament.

And they doe fit one fpace lower from the Cloath of eftate in the Parliament houfe. See *Cromptons Courts, Fol.* 12. *a.*

By the Statute made *Anno* 23. *Hen.* 8. *Can.* 21. It is thus defaced, the Affent of the King by his Letters Patents vnder the great Seale of *England*, and figned with his hand and notefied in his abfence to the Lords of the Parliament, and Commons affembled in the higher houfe, is and euer was of as good force and ftrength as if the perfon of the King had bin there prefent: and had aflented openly and publikely to the fame. And fuch Royall affent as is aforefaid fhall be taken, for good and effectuall to euery intent without any ambiguity of Cuftome or vfage to the contrary notwithftanding.

In

In this Court is attending, The Lord Chancellor of *England*, or the Lord Keeper of the great Seale, or some other sage man as the King shall choose: By whom the King doth shew his mind to the Lords. And hee doth put them in remembrance of those things which are to bee treated there before the Lords, who if hee bee no Baron, or Peere of the Realme, fitteth neare the King behind the cloath of Estate, And is as the Speaker of the vpper house of Parliament.

In the 31. yeare of *Hen.* 8. *Can.* 10. Intituled an act concerning placing of the Lords in the Parliament Chamber, and other assemblies and conferences of Counsell, It is enacted as followeth. *For asmuch as in all great Counsells and Congregations of men, hauing sundry degrees in the Common wealth, It is very requisite and conuenient, that an order be had and taken for the placing and setting of such persons as are bound to resort to the same; To the intent that they knowing their places, may vse the same without displeasure or let of the Councell: Wherefore the Kings most Royall Maiestie, although it appertaineth to his Prerogatiue Royall to giue such honor, places and reputation to his Councellors and other his subiects as shall seeme best to his most excellent Maiestie, Hee is neuerthelesse pleased and contented for an order to be had and taken in this his most high Court of Parliament, That it shall bee inacted by authoritie of the same, in manner and forme as hereafter followeth.*

First,

First, it is enacted by authority aforesaid, that no person or persons of what estate, degree or condition soeuer he or they be of (except onely the Kings Children) shall at any time hereafter attempt or presume to sit, and haue place at any side of the Cloath of State, in the Parliament Chamber, neither of th' one hand of the Kings highnesse, nor on the other : whether the Kings Maiestie be there personally present, or absent. And for as much as the Kings Maiestie is iustly and lawfull supreame head in Earth, of the Church of England, *vnder God. And for the exercise of the said most royall Dignitie and Office, hath made* Thomas Lord Cromwell, *and Lord priuie Seale, his Vicegerent, for good and due ministration of Iustice to be had and vsed in all Causes and Cases touching the Ecclesiasticall Iurisdiction, and for the godly reformation and redresse of all Errors, Heresies, and abuses in the same Church : It is therefore enacted by authoritie aforesaid, That the said Lord* Cromwell, *hauing the said Office of Vicegerent, and all other persons hauing the said Office of Vicegerent, And all other persons who shall hereafter haue the said Office of the grant of the Kings Highnesse, his heires and Successors shall sit and be placed as well in this present Parliament, as in all Parliaments whatsoeuer hereafter to be holden, on the right side of the Parliament Chamber ; And on the same forme that the Archbishop of* Canterbury *sitteth vpon ; and aboue the said Archbishop and his Successors, And shall haue place in euery Parliament to assent or dissent, as other the Lords of the Parliament.*

And it is also enacted, that next to the said Vicegerent shall sit the Archbishops of Canterbury *and* Yorke, *and then next him on the same forme and side, the Bishop of* London, *and next to him on the same forme and side the Bishop of* Duresme *; and next to him, on the same forme and sides the Bishop of* Winchester : *And then all the other Bishops,*

of

of both Proninces of Canterbury *and* Yorke *shall sit and be placed on the same side after their ancienties, as it hath beene accustomed.*

And for as much as such persons as now haue, or hereafter shall happen to haue other great Offices of the Realme, That is to say, The Office of the Lord Chancellour, Lord Treasurer, Lord President of the Kings Councell, The Lord priuie Seale, The Great Chamberlaine of England, *The Marshall of* England, *The Lord Admirall, The Grand Master or Lord Steward of the Kings most honourable Houshold; The Kings Chamberlaine, and the Kings Secretary, haue not heretofore beene appointed and ordered for the placing and sitting in the Kings most high Court of Parliament, by reason of their Offices, It is therefore now ordered, and enacted by authority aforesaid, That the said Lord Chancellour, Lord Treasurer, the President of the Kings Counsell, and the Lord priuie Seale, being of the degrees of Barons, or aboue, shall set and be placed as well in this present Parliament, as in all other Parliaments hereafter to be holden in the left hand of the Parliament Chamber, on the higher part of the forme on the same side, aboue all Dukes (except onely such as shall be the Kings Sonne, the Kings Brother, the Kings Vnckle, the Kings Nephew, or the Kings Brothers or Sisters Sonnes.*

And it is also ordained, and enacted by authority aforesaid, That the great Chamberlaine, the Constable, the Marshall, the Lord Admirall, the Grand Master or Lord Steward, and the Kings Chamberlaine shall sit and be placed after the Lord priuie Seale, in manner and forme following, That is to say, euery of them shall sit and be placed aboue all other personages being of the same estate or degree, that they shall happen to be of; That is to say the Great Chamberlaine first, the Constable second, the Marshall third :

third : the Lord *Admirall fourth* : the *Grand Master*
or *Lord Steward fift* , and the *Kings Chamberlaine*
the *sixt.*

And it is also enacted by authority aforesaid, That the
the *Kings chiefe Secretary*, being of the degree of a *Baron*
of the *Parliament*, shall sit and be placed aboue and before all
other *Barons*, not hauing any of the *Offices* afore remembred,
And if he be a *Bishop*, That then he shall sit and be placed a-
boue all other *Bishops*, not hauing any of the *Offices* aboue remembred.

And it is also ordained and enacted by authority aforesaid, That all *Dukes* not before mentioned, *Marquisses*,
Earles, *Viscounts*, and *Barons*, not hauing any of the Offices aforesaid, shall sit and be placed after their ancientie, as
it hath beene accustomed.

And it is further enacted, that if any person or persons
which at any time hereafter shall happen to haue any of the
Offices aforesaid, of *Lord Chancellour*, *Lord Treasurer*,
Lord President of the Kings Counsell, *Lord priuie Seale*,
or *chiefe Secretary*, shall be vnder the degree of a Ba on of
the *Parliament* ; By reason whereof they haue no interest to
giue any assent or dissent in the said house : That then in euery such *Case*, such of them as shall happen to be vnder the
said degree of a *Baron*, shall sit and be placed at the vpper-
most part of the *Sackes*, in the middest of the *Parliament*
Chamber, either there to sit vpon one forme, or vpon the vp-
permost *Sucke* ; The one of them aboue the other in order as
is aboue rehearsed.

Be it also enacted by authoritie aforesaid, that in all
tryals of *Treason* by *Peeres* of this *Realme* : If any of the
Peeres that shall be called hereafter to be *Tryers* of such

Treason,

Treafon, fhall happen to haue any of the Offices aforefaid, That then they hauing fuch Offices, fhall fit and be placed according to their Offices, aboue all th'other Peeres that fhall be called to fuch tryals, in manner and forme as is aboue mentioned and rehearfed.

And it is alfo enacted by authority aforefaid; That as well in all Parliaments, as in the Starchamber, and in all other Affemblies, and Conferences of Councell: The Lord Chauncellour, the Lord Treafurer, the Lord Prefident, the Lord Priuie Seale, the Great Chamberlaine, the Conftable, the Marfhall, the Lord Admirall, the Grand Mafter or Lord Steward, the Kings Chamberlaine, and the Kings chiefe Secretary, fhall fit and be placed in fuch order and forme as is aboue rehearfed, and not in any other place, by authority of this prefent Act.

And in Sir *Edward Cokes* 11. part. *fo.*1. The caufe concerning prioritie of place in the vpper houfe of Parliament was as followeth, at the Parliament held the 39. *Eliz.* The cafe was thus:

Thomas Lawarre Knight, Lord *Lawarre*, fonne and heire of *William*, fonne and heire of *George*, brother and heire of *Thomas*, fonne and heire of *Thomas* Lord *Lawarre*, exhibited his Petition to the Queene to this effect, That whereas *Thomas* the Great-grand-father was called to Parliament by Writ of Summons 3. H. 8. and afterwards this *Thomas* the Great-grand-father dyeth; After whofe death, *Thomas* his fonne, was called to diuers Parliaments by writ of Summons. And afterwards by act of Parliament 3. E. 6. for diuers caufes in the faid Act mentioned, it was enacted, That the faid *William* during his life, fhould be difabled to claime or enioy any dignity or fuperiority, in any right, eftate, &c. by difcent, remainder, or otherwife. And afterwards
wards

wards the faid *Thomas* the fonne of *Thomas* dyeth ; after whofe death the faid *William* being difabled, was
not called to any Parliament, by writ of Summons till
Queene *Elizabeth* called him to Parliament by writ of
Summons, and fetteth as yongeft Lord of the Parliament : And afterwards he dieth, and now the faid *Tho-*
mas his fonne being called to Parliament by writ of
Summons, fueth to the Queene that he may haue place
in Parliament, of his Great-grand-father(that is to fay)
betweene the Lord *Berkley* and the Lord *Willoughby* of
Eresby : And the faid Petition was indorced in thefe
words ; Her Maieftie hath commanded mee to fig-
nifie to your good Lordfhips, that vpon the humble
fuite of the Lord *Lawarre,* Shee is pleafed that the
matter fhall be confidered and determined in the
Houfe.

Robert Cecill.

Which Petition being read in the vpper houfe of
Parliament : The confideration of this was referred and
committed to the Lord *Burley* , Lord Treafuror of
England, and diuers other Committies, who at his
Chamber at *Whitehall* heard the learned Councell on
both fides , in the prefence of the two chiefe Iuftices,
and diuers other Iuftices : And two obiections were
made againft the Lord *Lawarre :* firft, in fo much that
his Father was difabled by act of Parliament to claime
the dignity ; The Petitioner may not conuay by him
who was difabled, as heire to his Great-grand-father,
and by confequence he may not haue the place of his
Great-grand-father.

But it was refolued by all the Iudges, That there was
a difference betweene a perfonall and a Temporary
difability, and abfolute and perpetuall difability : As
whereas

whereas one is attainted of Treafon or Fellony; this is abfolute and perpetuall difability by corruption of blood, for any of his pofterity to claime any hereditamont in Fee fimple, either as heire to him, or any other : But difability by Parliament without any Attainder, to claime the dignitie for his life; That is Perfonall difability for his life onely, and his heires after his death may claime as heire to him, or any other Anceftor aboue him : The fecond obieĉion is, that the faid *William* hath accepted new Creation of the Queene; which dignity newly gained, difcendeth to the petitioner which may not waue : and for that the Petitioner may not haue other place then his Father had.

To this it was anfwered and refolued, that th'acceptance of a new Creation by the faid *William*, may not hurt the Petitioner, becaufe the faid *William* was at that time difabled, and in truth he was not *Baron*, but onely an Efquire; fo that when th'old and new dignity difcended together, th'old fhall be preferred : which refolution was well approued by all the Lords Committies, which was accordingly reported to all the Lords of the Parliament, and allowed by them all : wherupon it was ordered by the Lords, that the Queen fhould be acquainted with this by the Lord Keeper, which was done accordingly.

Whereupon at the faid Parliament, the Lord *Lawarre* in his Parliament Robes, was by the Lord *Zouch* fupplying the place of the Lord *Willoughby*, within age at that time; And the Lord *Berkley* alfo in his Robes, brought into the houfe, and placed in his faid place (that is to fay) next after the Lord *Berkley*, *Garter* King at Armes attending vpon him, and doing his Office.

In the vpper houfe of Parliament doth fit the Iuftices vpon facks of Wooll, *in medir Camere*, who are
called

called thither by the Kings Writ, *qued perfonaliter inter fitis nobifcum ac cum ceteris de confilio noftro prediſtis negotiis, traſtat veſtrumque confilium impenfurum* : And this *negotia* be *Ardua & vrgentia negotia Regni, &c.* And their oath amongſt other things is, that they ſhall Counſell the King truely in his buſineſſe, but they haue no voyce among the Lords.

If the Reader be deſirous to ſee particular caſes happening in Parliament, wherin the opinion of the Iudges there had beene recreated : And how their opinions deliuered in Parliament ought to be regarded, he may read at large in *Egertons poſt-nati. fol.* 16. *& ſequentum.*

If a Writ of Error be brought in Parliament vpon a Iudgement giuen in *Kings-Bench* ; The Lords of the Higher houſe onely, without the Commons are to examine the Errors ; and that is by th'aduice and counſell of the Iudges, who are to informe them what the Law is, and ſo to direct them in their Iudgement : and if the Iudgement be reuerſed, then commandement is to be giuen to the Lord Chancellour to doe execution accordingly. And ſo was done in the 7. of R.2. in a Writ brought in Parliament by the Deane and Chapter of *Litchfeild,* againſt the Prior and Couent of *Neuport Pannell,* as appeareth by the Record. And if the Iudgement be affirmed, then the Court of Kings Bench are to proceed to execution of the Iudgement, as appeareth in *Howerdewes* caſe 1.H.7.*fo.*19.

But it is to be noted, that in all ſuch Writs of Errors, The Lords are to proceede according to the Law; and for their iudgement therein, they are informed and guided by the Iudges, and doe not follow their owne opinions, or diſcretions. See *Egertons poſt-nati. fol.* 23.

There doth alſo ſit the Secretaries of eſtate, who are

to

to anfwer fuch Letters or things paffed in the Councell whereof they haue the keeping : And with them the Mafter of the Roles ; But they haue no voice in Parliament, if they be not of the degree of a Baron.

Note by *Kirby*, Clerks of the Roles of the Parliament : It is thus in the Bookes of the Law, the 33. H. 6. ca. 17. If a Bill come firft to the Commons, and they doe paffe it ; then the vfe is to indorfe it in this forme, *Soyt Bayle a feignoures:* And then if the Lords nor King doe not alter the Bill, then it fhall be inroled by the Clerke of the Parliament ; and if the Bill paffe, then it fhall be Inrolled, but if it be a particular Bill, then it fhall be filed vpon *filaces*, and that fhall fuffice, vnleffe the partie whom it particularly concernes will fue to haue it Inroled, that it may be Inroled to be fure.

If the Lords will alter a Bill, fent to them from the Lower houfe, in a thing that may ftand with the Bill, they may doe fo without remanding to the Commons. And if the Commons doe grant pomage for foure yeares, and the Lord will grant it but for two yeares, this Bill fhall not be deliuered againe to the Commons : But if the Commons doe grant but onely for two yeares, and the Lords doe grant it for foure yeares, then the Bill muft be remanded to the Commons, and in that cafe the Lord muft make a Scedule of their intent, or elfe indorced in this forme, *Les feigneures fe affent pur durar pur quater anne :* And when the Commons haue the Bill againe ; if they doe not affent to it, then it is no Act or Statute ; and if the Commons doe confent, then they doe indorfe their anfwer vpon the Margent within the Bill in a certaine forme.

And then it fhall be deliuered vnto the Clerke of the Parliament, *vt fupra.*

If the Bill be firft deliuered to the Lords, and the Bill doth

doth paſſe them, they vſe not to make any indorſe-
ment, but to ſend the Bill to the Commons; and if it
paſſe them alſo, it is vſed to be thus indorſed, *Les Com-
mones fout aſſentant, &c.* And therefore if *Iohn* at *Stile*
be attainted of Treſpaſſe by Parliament, if he doe not
come in by ſuch a day, he ſhall forfeit ſuch a ſum. And
the Lords doe giue a longer day, if it doe not come to
the Commons againe, it is no Act or Statute, becauſe
it was not remaunded againe to the Commons after the
enlargement of the day giuen by the Lords.

Euery Bill that doth paſſe the Parliament in both
Houſes, ſhall haue relation to the firſt day of the Parliament: And the vſe is, not to make mention what
day the Bill was deliuered into the Parliament: If no
day be ſpecially appointed by the Statute, when it ſhall
Commence: As if one Parliament be holden by diuers
prorogations, *Plowdens Commentaries. fol. 79. a. 6.*

If a Parliament doe Commence before Penticoſt, and
hath continuance after Penticoſt, and the Commons
doe agree to a Bill after Penticoſt, and in the ſame doe
giue day till Penticoſt next comming; And the Lords
doe ſo alſo, becauſe the Bill ſhall haue relation to the
firſt day of the Parliament. Therefore if it be not pre-
uented, it ſhall be taken for that Penticoſt that is paſt
at that Seſſions, whereas th'intent of the Lords and
Commons was, that it ſhould be a future Penticoſt after that Penticoſt mentioned in the Bill. See *Brookes
Prerogatiues and Parliaments.* 4.

The Barons in the vpper houſe of Parliament may
(in ſome caſes) giue their voyces by procuracie, not ſo
in the Lower houſe: And thoſe Proctors muſt be Barons, and of the Higher houſe of Parliament. But in
the Lower houſe of Parliament it is otherwiſe, for the
Clarke of the Parliament take the notice of the moſt
hands or voyces ſounding at once. And therefore if

their

their aſſent be iſſuable, the Clerke may ſay *Per maio-
rem-numerum generalis.* So in caſe of Election of
Crowner or a Knight of the Parliament. See *Plowdens
Commentaries.* 126. *a.*

All the priuiledges which doe belong to thoſe of the
Lower houſe of Parliament : *a fortiori* doe appertaine
to all the Lords of the vpper houſe ; for their perſons
are not onely free from arreſts during the Parliament,
but during their liues, neuertheleſſe th'originall cauſe
is by reaſon they haue place and voyce in Parliament :
And this is manifeſt by expreſſe authorities grounded
vpon excellent reaſons in the Bookes of Law.

And if a Baron, Viſcount, Earle, Marqueſſe or Duke
of *England* bring any action reall or perſonall, and the
defendant pleadeth in abatement of the Writ, That he
is no Baron, Viſcount, Earle, &c. And thereupon the
demaundant or plaintiffe pleadeth in abatement of the
Writ, and taketh iſſue ; This Iſſue ſhall not be tryed
by a Iury, but by the Records of the Parliaments, whether he or his anceſtors, whoſe heire he is, were called to ſerue there as a Peere, or one of the Nobi-
lity of the Realme, See Sir *Edw. Cokes* 6. *part.* 53. & 7.
part. fo. 17. *a.*

In the ancient *Britanes* and *Saxons* Kings dayes, the
Archbiſhops and Biſhops were called to their Parliaments, or other aſſemblies of State; which was done
not ſo much in reſpect of their tenures, for in thoſe
dayes all their tenures were *Francki Almonage,* but eſ-
pecially becauſe the Lawes and Councels of Men were
then moſt currant and commendable, and had a more
bleſſed iſſue and ſucceſſe, when they were grounded
vpon the feare of God, the root and beginning of wiſedome. And therefore our wiſe and religious Anceſtors
called thither thoſe chiefe and principall perſons of
the Clergie, who by their place and poſſeſſion, by their
graui-

grauities, learning and wifedome might beſt aduiſe them, what was the Law of God, his acceptable will and pleaſure : That they might from their humane Lawes anſwerable, or at the leaſt not contrary or repugnant thereunto. Neuertheleſſe ſhortly after the *Norman* Conqueſt, the Conquerour altered the tenure of the Biſhoprickes, not without ſome complaint and griefe of the Clergie, as it is mentioned in *Matthew Paris, Anno* 1070.

And in the Conſtitutions of *Clarendon*, in the time of H. 2. *Anno* 1164. It is expreſſed in the eleauenth Article.

Thereby we ſee the preſence of the Biſhops in Parliament, in reſpect of their Baronies, *quouſque Terueniatur ad diminicionem, &c.* for ſo euen vnto our times, when queſtion is had of the Attainder of any Peere, or other in Parliament ; the Archbiſhops and Biſhops depart the higher houſe, and doe make their Proctors ; for by the decrees of the Church, they may not be Iudges of life and death. Euer ſince the Conqueſt the Archbiſhops and Biſhops haue no title to haue place and voyce in Parliament, but onely in reſpect of their Temporall Baronies.

And it is to be obſerued, that although of latter times the vſe and manner of penning of Statutes, is that it is enacted by the Lords Spirituall and Temporall, and the Commons in the ſame aſſembled : yet the ancient forme was not ſo, which you may ſee exemplified in Sir *Edw. Cokes* 8. *part. fo.* 19.

And good Acts of Parliaments may be made, though the Archbiſhops and Biſhops would not conſent thereunto : for a Statute was made *Anno* 1196. by the King, the Barons, and the Commons (*Clero excluſo* :) And this was at a Parliament holden at Saint *Edmundsbury*, in the raigne of E. 1. as it is reported by *Iewell* Biſhop of

of *Salisbury* againſt *Harding, fo.*620. And in the Pro-
uice of *Mirton,* in the time of H.8. 1272. a matter was
moued of baſtardy, touching the legitimation of Ba-
ſtards, borne before Marriage; where it is ſaid, That
the Statute did paſſe entirely with the Lords temporall,
againſt the wils of the Lords ſpirituall : which Statute
is in the Bookes in the 20. yeare of H.8.3.*c.9.*

And in the 11. yeare of R.2.ca.3. It is enacted, that
the Appeales, Purſuits, Accuſements, Proceſſe, Iudge-
ments, and Executions, made and giuen in this preſent
Parliament, be approued, affirmed, and eſtabliſhed, as
a thing duely made for the weale and profit of the King
our Soueraigne Lord, and of all the Realme, notwith-
ſtanding that the Lords ſpirituall and their procurators
did abſent themſelues out of the Parliament, the time
of the ſaid Iudgement giuen, for the honeſty and ſalua-
tion of their eſtates, as it is contained in a proteſtation
made by the Lords ſpirituall, and their procurators deliuered in this preſent Parliament.

See *Kelbaucyes* Booke, *fo.* 184. in the 7.H.8. The Iuſtices did ſay, that our Soueraigne Lord the King may
well hold his Parliament by him and his temporall
Lords, and by the Commons alſo without the ſpirituall Lords, for the ſpirituall Lords haue not any place
in the Parliament Chamber, by reaſon of their ſpiritu-
alties , but onely by reaſon of their temporall poſ-
ſeſſions.

The Soueraigne power of this high Court of Parliament is this; That albeit the Kings Maieſtie
hath many great priuiledges and prerogatiues, yet many things there are not effectuall in Law, to paſſe vnder
the great Seale by the Kings Charter without Parliament : as vpon this point it was reſolued by all the
Iudges in the Princes caſe, That the Dukedome of
Cornewall, &c. did not, nor could paſſe from E.3. by
his

his Carter made in Parliament: That his Sonne and heire apparant, and to his heires informe, as it was intended and made in *Anno* 11. of his raigne. But of necessitie it was, and so was done by authority of Parliament: which Case is notable and worth the reading. See Sir *Edw. Cokes* 8. *part. fo.* and his 7. *part. fo.*7.*a.* The King by his Letters Patents may make a deuision, but cannot naturalise him to all purpofes, as an Act of Parliament may doe; for the Kings Charter cannot make any hereditable, in this cafe, that by the common Lawes cannot inherit. And herewith agreeth the 36. of H.8. *Denizon Brooke.*

Bracton in the beginning of his fecond Booke, faith; *Nihil aliud potest Rex in terris cum sit dei minister & vicarius quam quod de iure potest:* and a little after, *Itaque Potestas sua est Iuris non iniuria & sicut sit author Iuris non debet inde Iniuriam nasci occasio vnde iura nascuntur.*

And it appeareth in *Fitzharberts natura Breuium* 222 in the Writ *ad quam damnum*, that euery grant of the King or gift, hath his condition expressed or imployed, as by the Law annexed to it; *Itaque quod per --- adonationem illam patria magis solito non oneretur sui grauetur.*

And therefore it was refolued by all the Iudges 4. *Iacobi*, that they who digge for falt-Peter, may not digge within the Mansion houfe of any Subiect, without his affent, for the manifeft inconueniences that thereby may grow to the owner of the houfe. See Sir *Ed.Coke* 11.part.82.

Alfo the Commiffion to be made, the Purueyors for Timber, for the Kings vfe; yet they cannot by that authority marke Timber Trees growing vpon any mans Freehold: for that is prohibited by *Magna Carta*, *ca.*21. *nos nec balliui nostri nec alij capemus bofcum alic-*

num

num ad caſtra vel ad alia agenda noſtra niſi per voluntatem
cuius boſcus ille fuerit.

A Commiſſion was awarded to take ſinging Boyes
in Cathedrall Churches, or in other places whereſuch
are inſtructed, for the furniſhing of the Kings Chap-
pell ; theſe generall words by conſtruction ſhall haue a
reaſonable vnderſtanding : That is to ſay, ſuch children
who be taught to ſing, thereby to acquire or get their
liuings, ſuch may be taken for the Kings ſeruice ; But
the ſonne of a Gentleman, or any other, who is taught
to ſing for his recreation, ornament, or delight, may
not be taken againſt his will, or againſt the will of
his Parents, or friends : and ſo it was reſolued by
all the Iudges, and whole Court of Starre-Chamber
43. *Eliz.*

If a man be attainted of Felony or Treaſon, by Ver-
dict, Outlary, Confeſſion, &c. his blood is corrupted :
which is a perpetuall and abſolute diſabilitie for him or
his poſteritie, to claime any hereditament in Feeſim-
ple, either as heire to him or any Anceſtor *Paramount*
him ; and he ſhall not be reſtored to his blood without
Parliament : And the King may giue to any attainted
perſon his life, by his Charter of Parliament. See
Stamfords pleas 195. For the King cannot alter the
Common Law, or the generall cuſtomes of the Realme,
ſuch as the diſcent of *Gauill* kinde, *Borough, Engliſh*,
or ſuch like, without Parliament. See *Brooks Preroga-*
tiue 15. & 11.H.4.c.73.

And it is ſet downe for a rule ; That if a King haue
a Kingdome by diſcent there, ſeeing by the Law of that
Kingdome he doth inherit that Kingdome, He cannot
change thoſe Lawes of himſelfe, without conſent of
Parliament.

Forteſcugh alſo ſaith in his *9.c. fo.* 25.6. If the power of the King ouer his Subiects were Royall onely, and
not

not politicke, then he might change the Lawes of the Realme, and charge his Subiects with Tallages and other Burdens, without their confent. And fuch is the dominion of the Ciuill Law purports, when they fay, *quod principi placuit legis habet vigorem.* But by the Lawes of this Kingdome, the King cannot by his Proclamation alter the Law ; But the King may make Proclamation that he fhall incurre the indignation of his Maieftie, that withftanding it. And by his abfolute authority, the King may commit any one to prifon, during his pleafure. See *Stamford* 72. But the penalty of not obtaining his Proclamation, may not be vpon paine of forfeiture of his Goods, his Lands, or his life without Parliament. See *Cromptons Courts* 14. *a. &* 16.6. *fed omnes non capit hoc verbum :* for they of another profeffion in Law, fay, that of thefe two, one muft needes be true, that either the King is aboue the Parliament, that is the pofitiue Law of the Kingdome ; or elfe, that he is an abfolute King. *Areft. leb. Pliēt. c.* 16. And therefore though it be a mercifull pollicie, and alfo a politicke mercy, not alterable without great perill : And to make Lawes by the confent of the whole Realme, becaufe no one party fhall haue caufe to complaine of a partialitie ; yet fimply to binde the King to or by thofe Lawes, were repugnant to the nature and conftitution of an abfolute Monarchy.

In fome fpeciall cafes there fomctimes may be liking of Subiects without land of poffcffion, as in the gouernment which *Mofes* had ouer the children of *Ifrael,* in the Wilderneffe, and in the cafe which Sir *Iohn Popham,* the late Lord chiefe Iuftice, did put in the Parliament ; If a King and his Subiects be driuen out of his Kingdome by his Enemies, yet notwithftanding he continueth ftill King ouer his Subiects, and they ftill are bound to him by their bonds of allegiance, where-

foeuer

foeuer they be : But he cannot be a King without Subiects, for that were *Imperium inbellans & Rex & Sub-
dita funt relatiua.*

I beleeue *Salomon* that faith, *per me reges regnant &*
Principes iuſta dicerunt. And I make no douot, but as
God ordained Kings, and hath giuen Lawes to Kings
themfelues, fo he hath authorized and giuen power to
Kings to giue Lawes to their Subiects : and fo Kings
did firſt make Lawes, and then ruled by their Lawes,
and altered and changed their Laws from time to time,
as they faw occafion, for the good of themfelues and of
their Subiects.

By the Premiffes it appeareth, that Acts of Parliament
and Statutes are made in this high Court of Parliament
by the King, with the confent of the Commons, or by
the greater part of them, for fo faith *Littleton* in the
15. E. 4. fo. 2. a.

In the Parliament, if the greater part of the Knights
of the fheere doe affent to the making of an Act of
Parliament, and the leffer part will not agree to it, yet
this is a good Act or Statute, to laſt *in perpetum*: And
that the Law of *Maior pars* is fo in all Counfels, Elections, &c. both by the rules of the Common Law and the
Ciuill, and common Law alfo.

In this Court of Parliament, they doe make new pofitiue Lawes or Statutes, and fometimes they inlarge
fome of them, as vnto them feemeth good : and it is
good counfell, that in making of Lawes, *quod eius fieri*
poffit, quamplurima legibus definientur quam paciſſima
vera Iudicis arbitrio relinquantur. Yet for fo much as
euery confiderable circumſtance cannot be forefeene
at the time of the making of the Law ; for, *rerum pro-*
greffus oftendunt multa quo in mitio Precaueri feu proui-
deri non poffunt. Therefore by the very intent of the
makers of the Statute, they doe many times leaue to be
fupplied

ſuppoſed by the diſcretion of th'executioner of the Law, that thing which was not conuenienily comprehended before hand, by the wiſedome of the Authors of the ſame : for the expounding of the Lawes doth ordinarily belong to the reuerend Iudges, and in caſe of greateſt difficultv of importance, to the high Court of Parliament. See *Plowdens Commentaries, fo. 363. a. 3 *4. & 365.*

And the Iudges doe ſay that they may not make any interpretation againſt the expreſſe words of the Statute, where th'intent of the makers of the Law doe appeare to the contrary, and where no inconuenience by the Statute ſhall enſue : for in ſuch caſes *A verbis legum non eſt recedendu.*

But to exemplifie all the ſeuerall kinds and formes of penning them, and the words of them taken and conſtrued, ſometimes by execution, ſometimes by reſtriction, ſometimes by implication, ſometimes by diſiunction, ſometimes a diſiunctiue for a copulatiue, ſometimes a copulatiue for a diſiunctiue, the preſent tence for the future, the future for the preſent, ſometimes by equitie out of the reach of the words, ſometimes taken in a contrary ſence, ſometimes ſingularly, as *Continens* pro *content,* and ſuch like, will aske a volume by it ſeite, and in my opinion is not incident to this diſcourſe of the *Iuriſdiction of the high Court of Parliament.*

G   Here-

Hereunto is annexed

A briefe Abſtract of the worthi-
neſſe of, and ſome memorable matters done by PARLAMENTS in
this Kingdome of
ENGLAND.

BY *Parliaments all the wholeſome fundamentall Lawes of this Land were and are eſtabliſhed and confirmed.*

By Act of Parliament the Popes Power and Supremacie, and all ſuperſtition and Idolatry are abrogated, aboliſhed and baniſhed out of this Land.

By Act of Parliament Gods true Religion, worſhip and ſeruice are maintained and eſtabliſhed

By Act of Parliament the two famous Vniuerſities of Cambridge *and* Oxford *haue many wholeſome and helpefull Immunities.*

By Parliament one Pierce Gaueſton, *a great fauourite and notable miſleader of K. Ed. 2. was remoued, baniſhed, and afterwards by the Lords executed.*

By Parliament Empſon *and* Dudley, *two notorius Polers of the Common-wealth, by exacting pe-*
nall

nall Lawes on the Subiects, were discouered, and afterwards executed.

By *Parliament the damnable Gunpowder-Treason (hatched in Hell) is recorded to be had in eternall Infamie.*

By *Parliament one Sir* Giles Mompeſſon, *a Moderne Caterpiller and poler of the Common-wealth, by exacting vpon Inholders, &c. was discouered, degraded from Knighthood, and banished by Proclamation.*

By *Parliament Sir* Francis Bacon, *made by King* Iames *Baron* Veralam *and Viſcount S.* Albanes, *and Lord Chancellour of* England, *very grieuous to the Common-wealth, by Bribery, was discouered and diſplaced.*

By *Parliament Sir* Iohn Bennit *Iudge of the Prerogatiue Court, pernicious to the Common-wealth in his place, was discouered and diſplaced.*

By *Parliament* Lyonell Cranfield *(sometimes a Merchant of* London) *made by* K. Iames *Earle of* Middleſex, *and Lord Treaſurer of* England, *hurtfull in his place to the Common-wealth, was discouered and diſplaced.*

By *Parliament one Sir* Francis Mitchell, *a iolly Iuſtice of Peace for* Middleſex *in the Suburbs of* London, *another notable Cankerworme of the Common-wealth, by corruption in exacting the penall Lawes vpon poore Alehouſe-keepers and Victuallers, &c. was discouered, degraded from Knighthood, and vtterly diſabled for being Iuſtice of Peace.*

By

By Parliament Spaines *late fraud was discoue-* *red, and by Act the two Treaties, with that perfidi-* *ous Nation, for the Match of the Prince, our now* *gracious King; and restitution of the Palatinate* *were dissolued and annihilated: both which had cost* *the King and his Subiects much monie, and much* *blood. We may remember that that sage Councellour* *of State Sir* William Cecill *Lord* Bnrleigh, *and* *Lord Treasurer of* England, *was oft times heard to* *say,* He knew not what an Act of Parliament *might not doe: which sage saying was approued* *by King* Iames, *and by his Maiestie alleaged in one* *of his published Speeches.*

Which being so, now the face of Christendome be- *ing at this present so torne and miserably maserated,* *and the Christian World distracted; the Gospell in* *all places, almost, persecuted, both Church and Com-* *mon-wealth, where the Gospell is professed, in all pla-* *ces beyond the Seas, lying a bleeding (as wee may* *say) and we our selues at home not without feare and* *danger. To conclude, what good may wee not hope* *and pray for by this present and other ensuing Par-* *liaments? the onely meanes to rectifie and remedy* *matters in Church and Common-wealth much a-* *misse.* Amen.

Viuat Rex
Floreat Regnum
Bene valeat Parlamentum.

FINIS.